This Tractor Coloring Book Belongs To :

____

This Book Published By Machine Coloring Books

These photos are designed
By Vecteezy.com

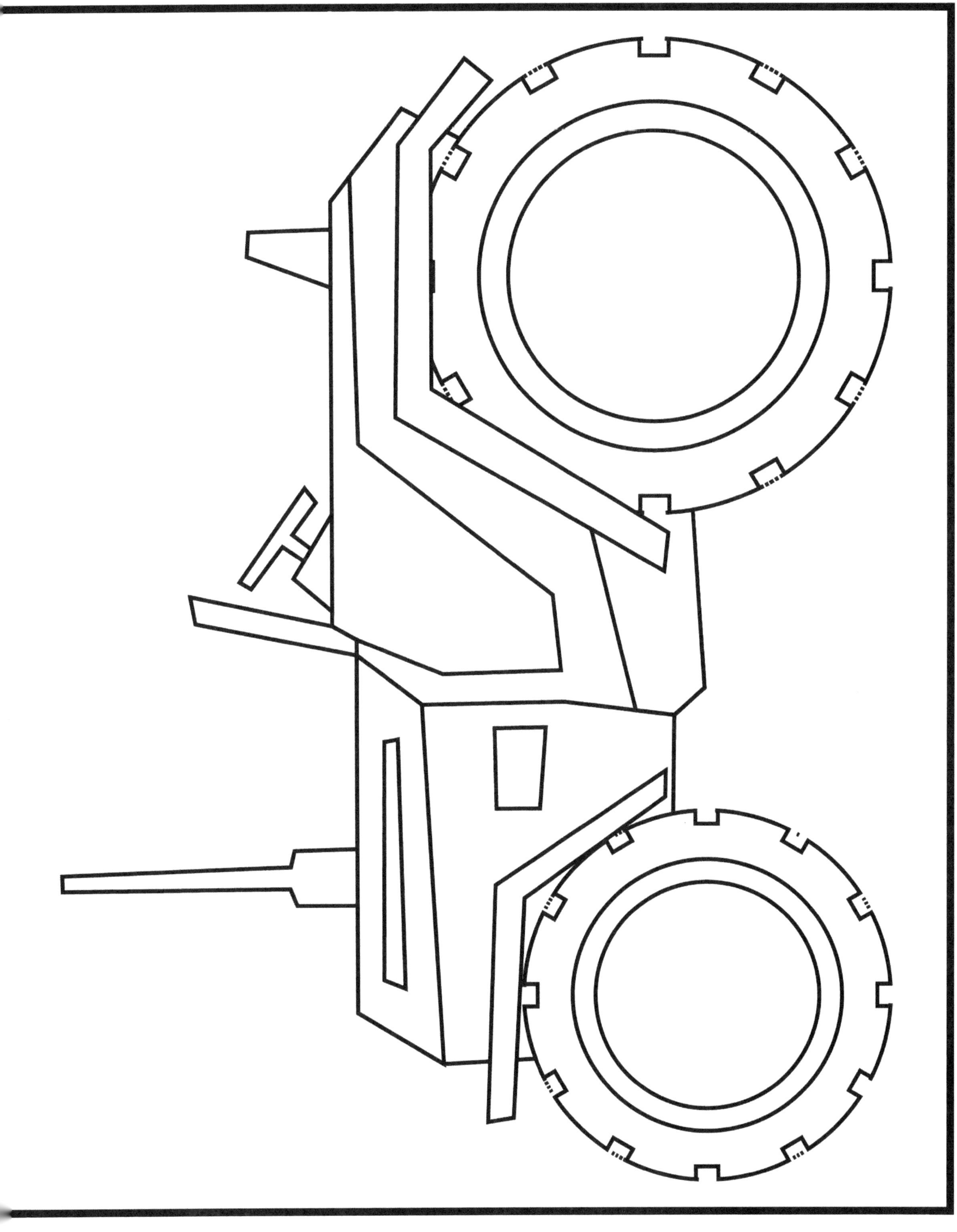

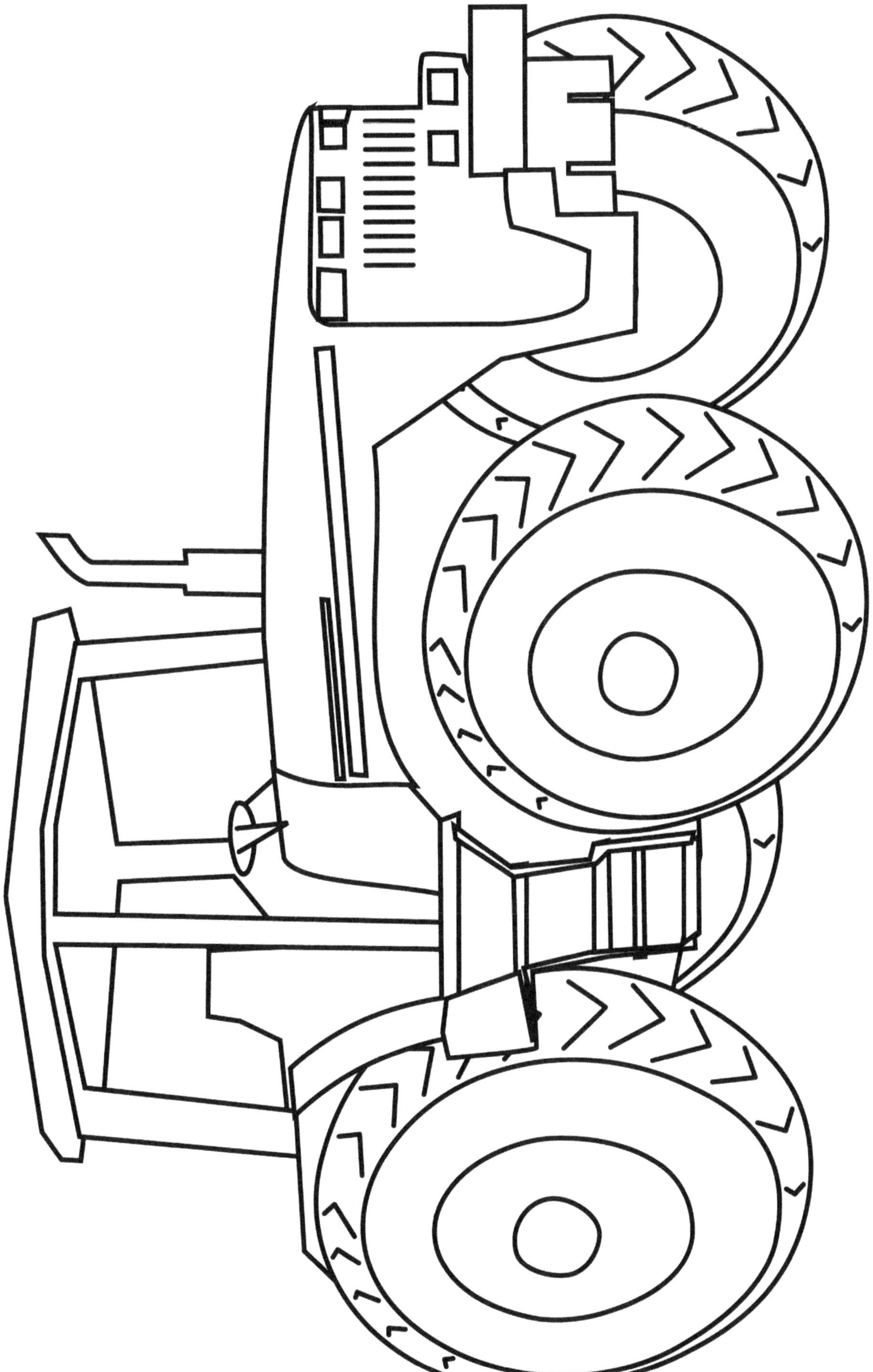

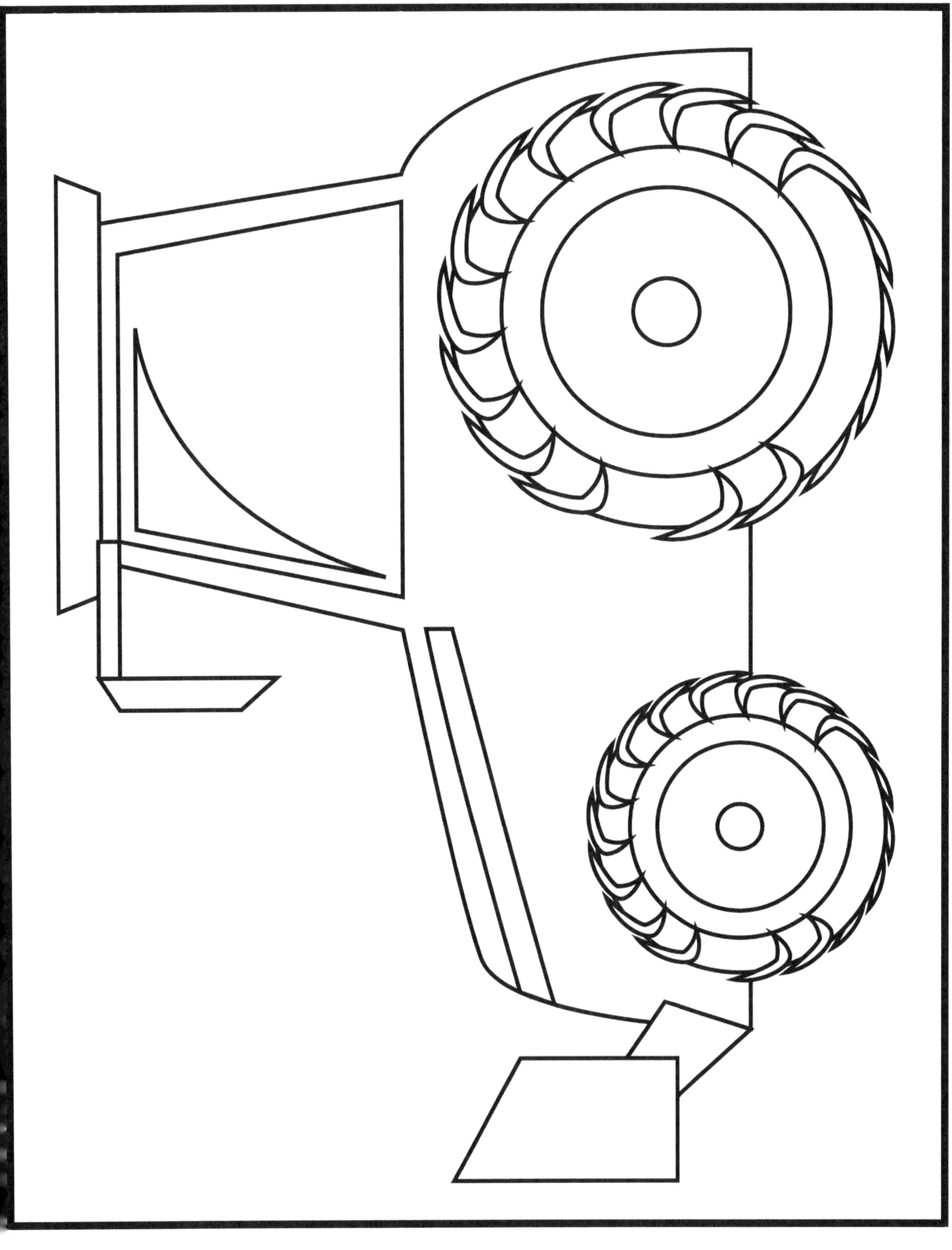

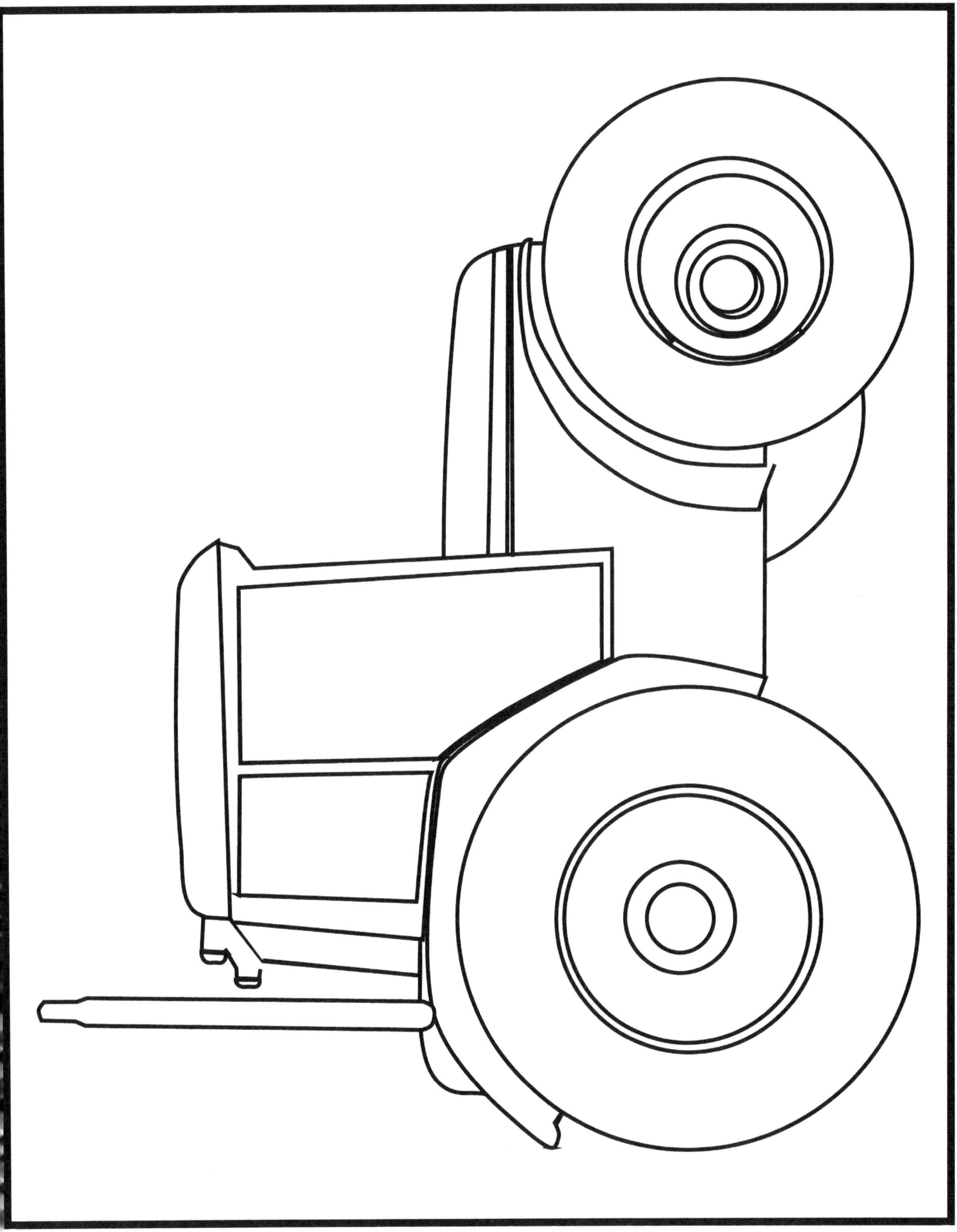

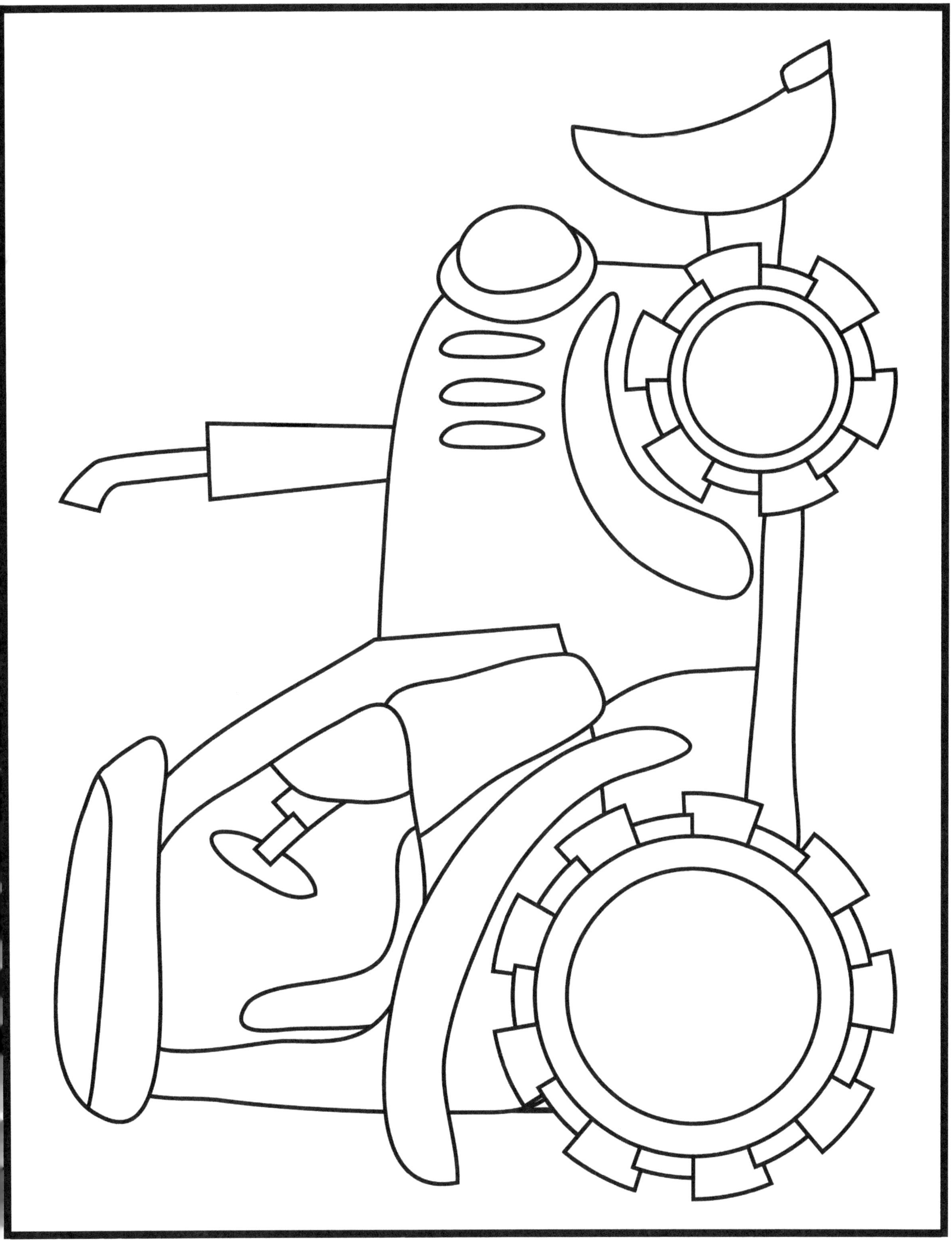

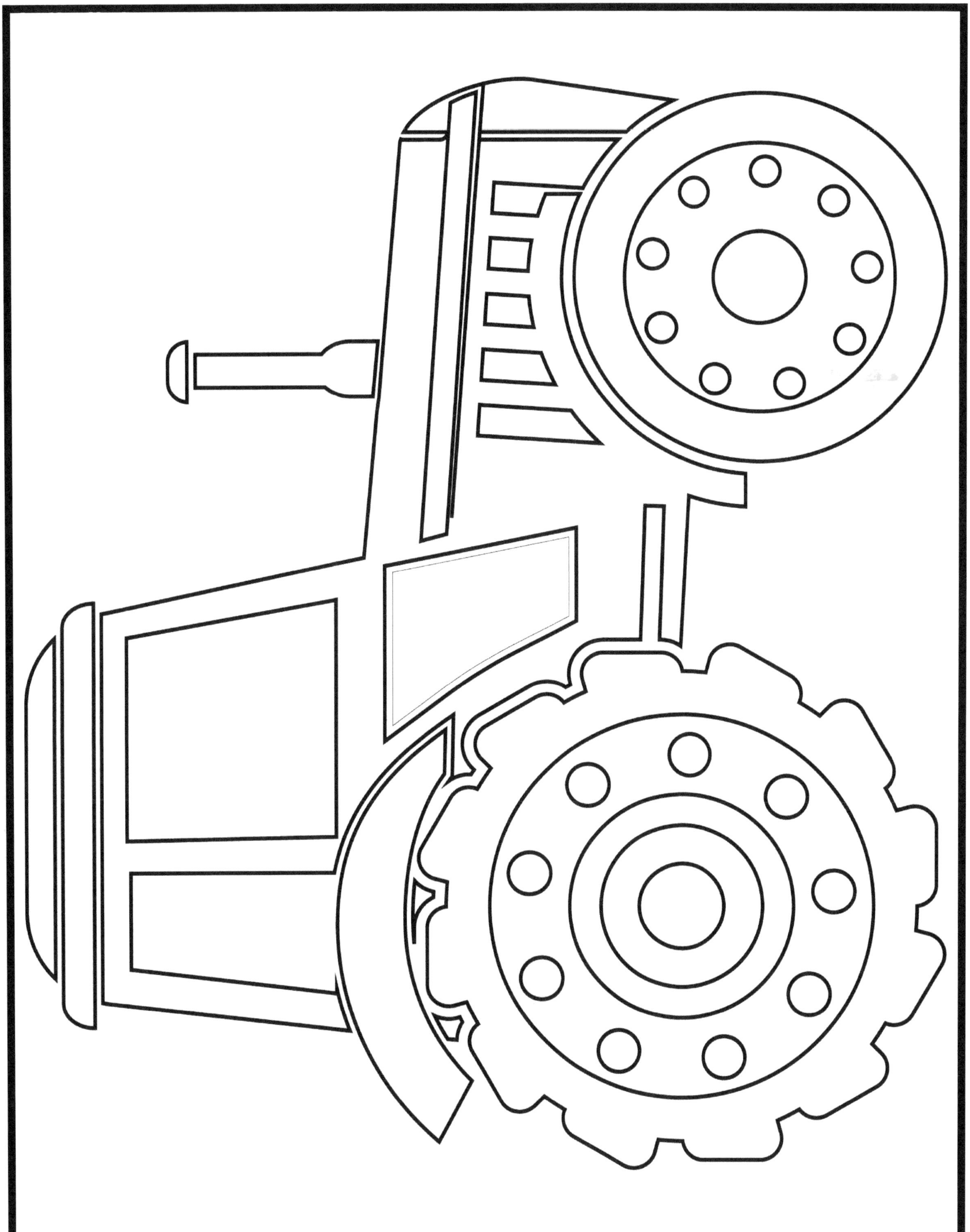

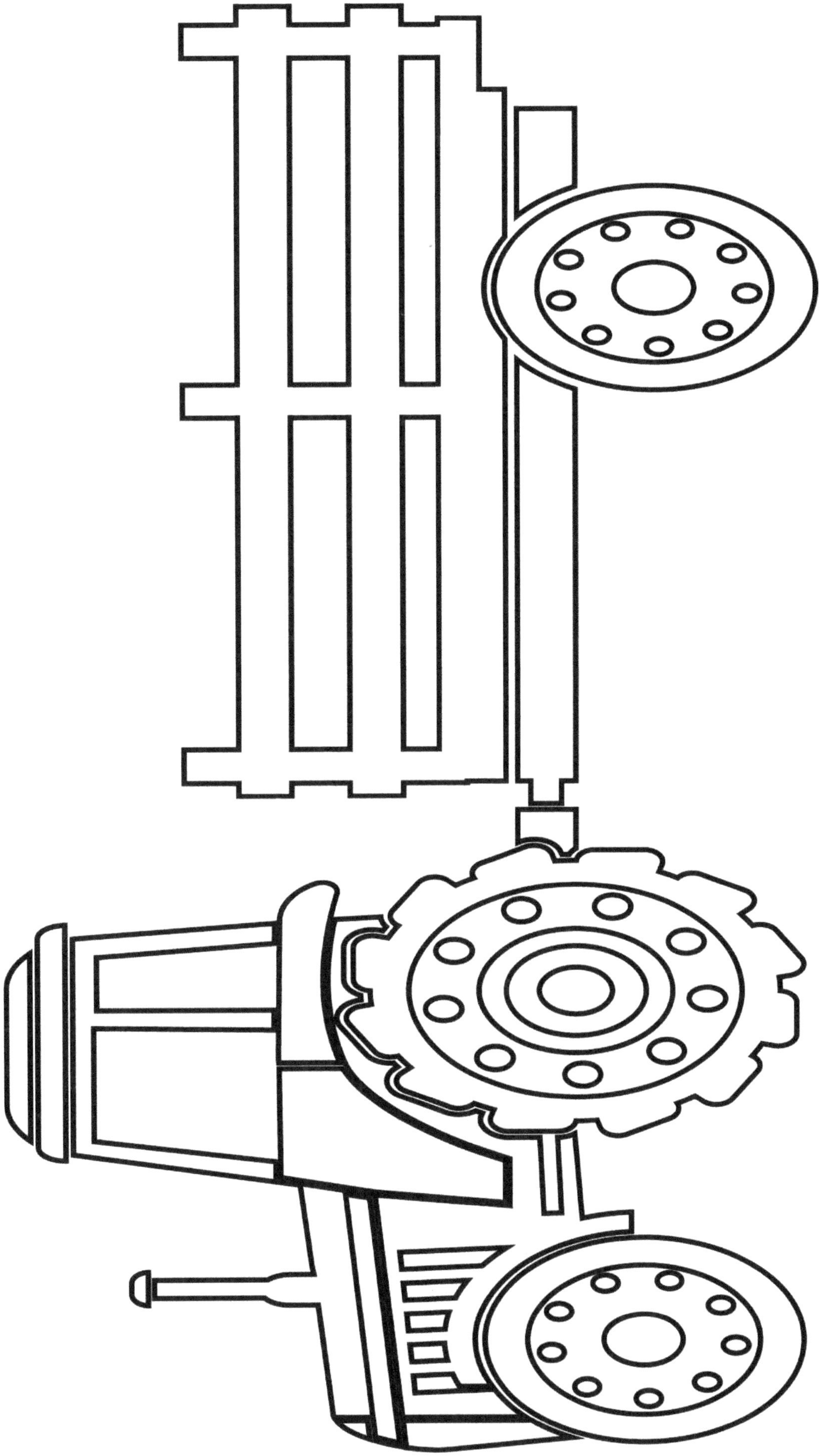

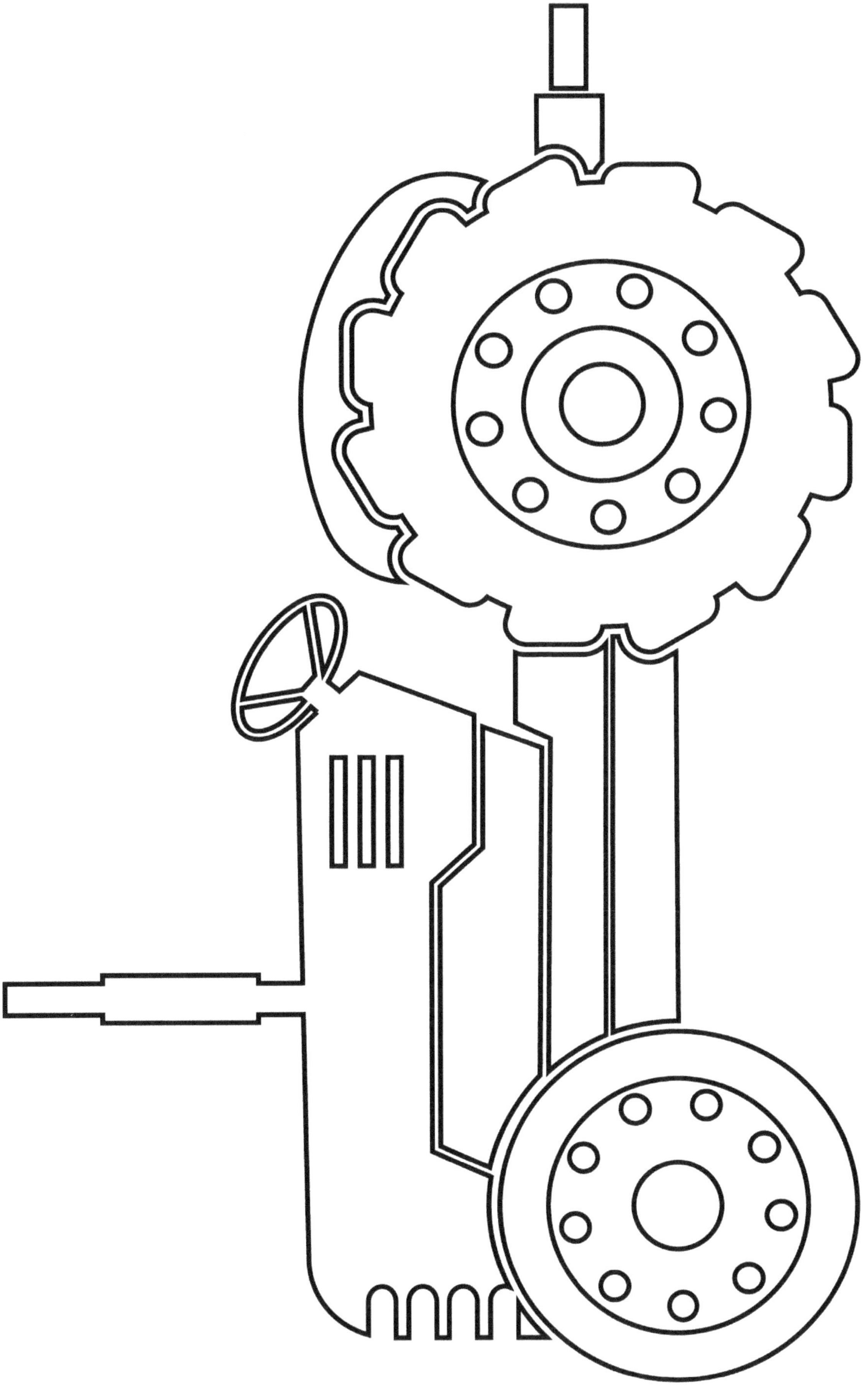

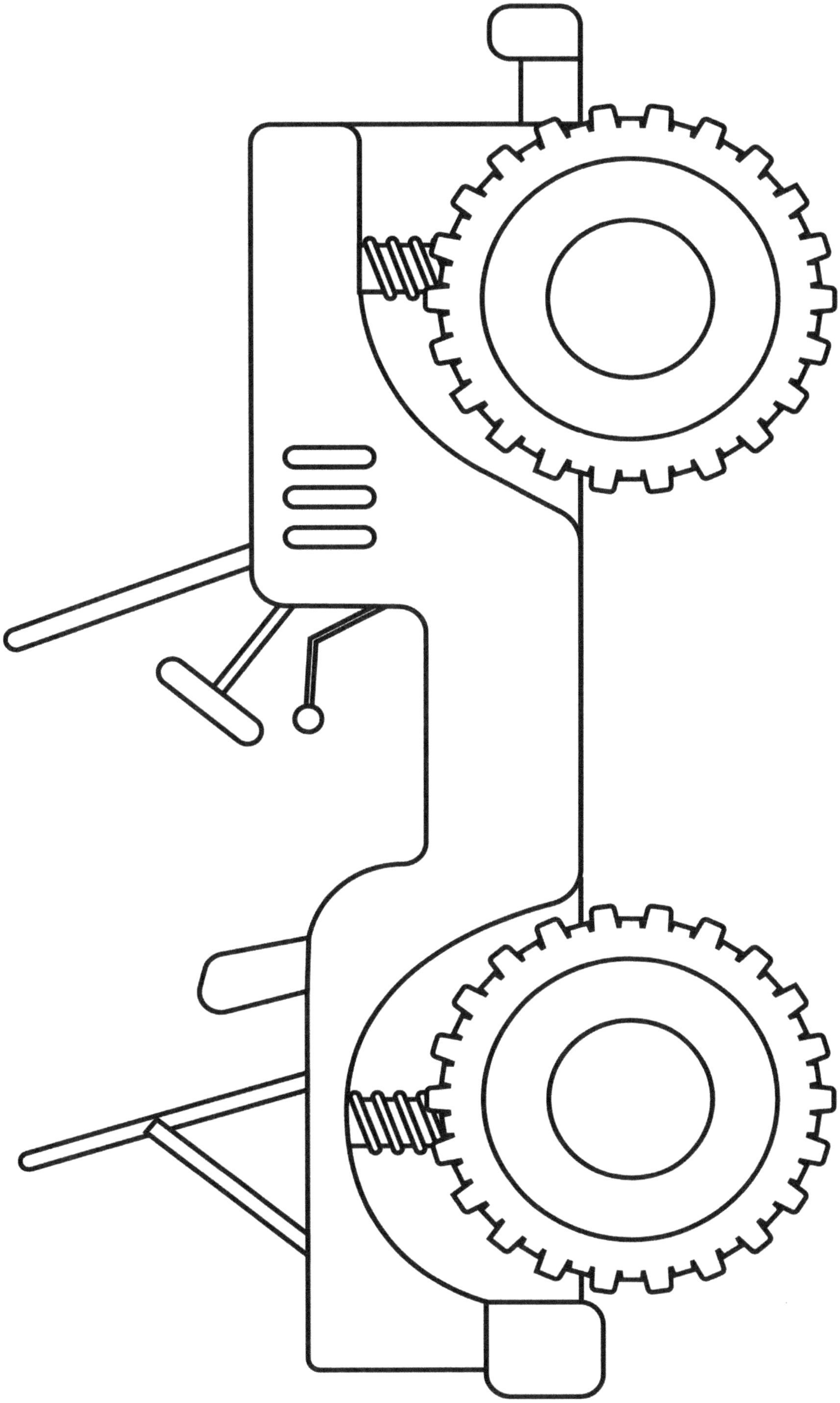

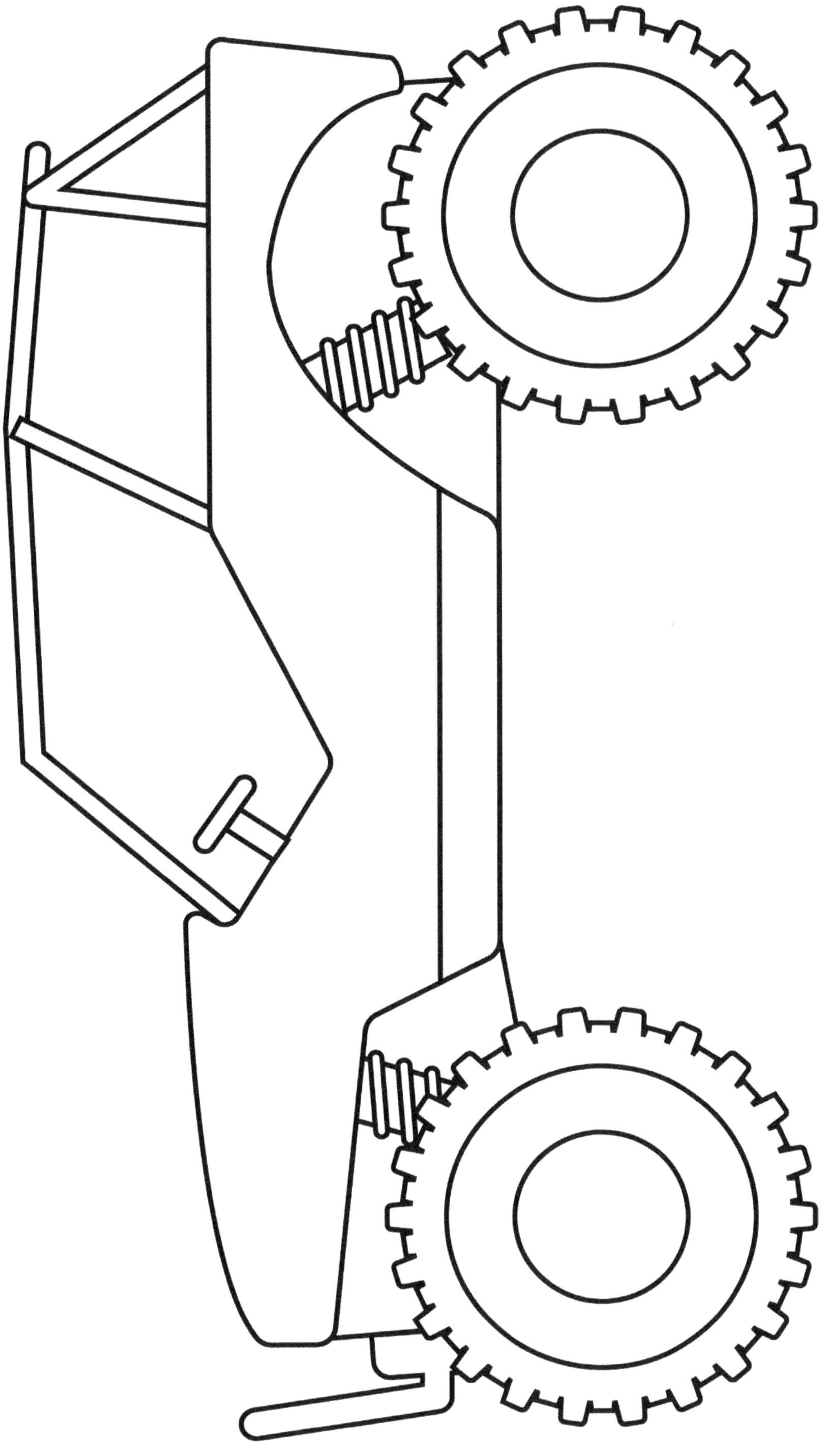

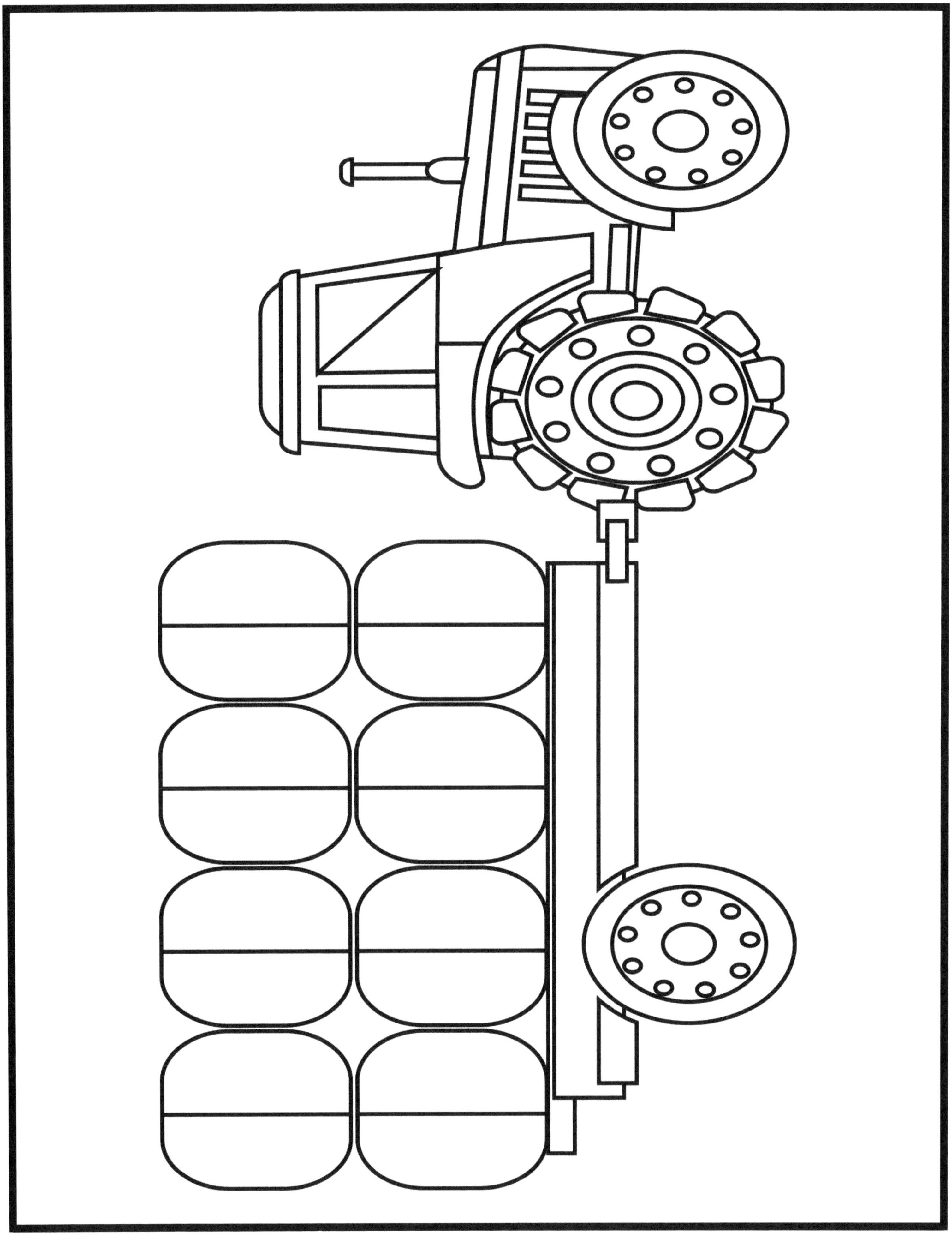

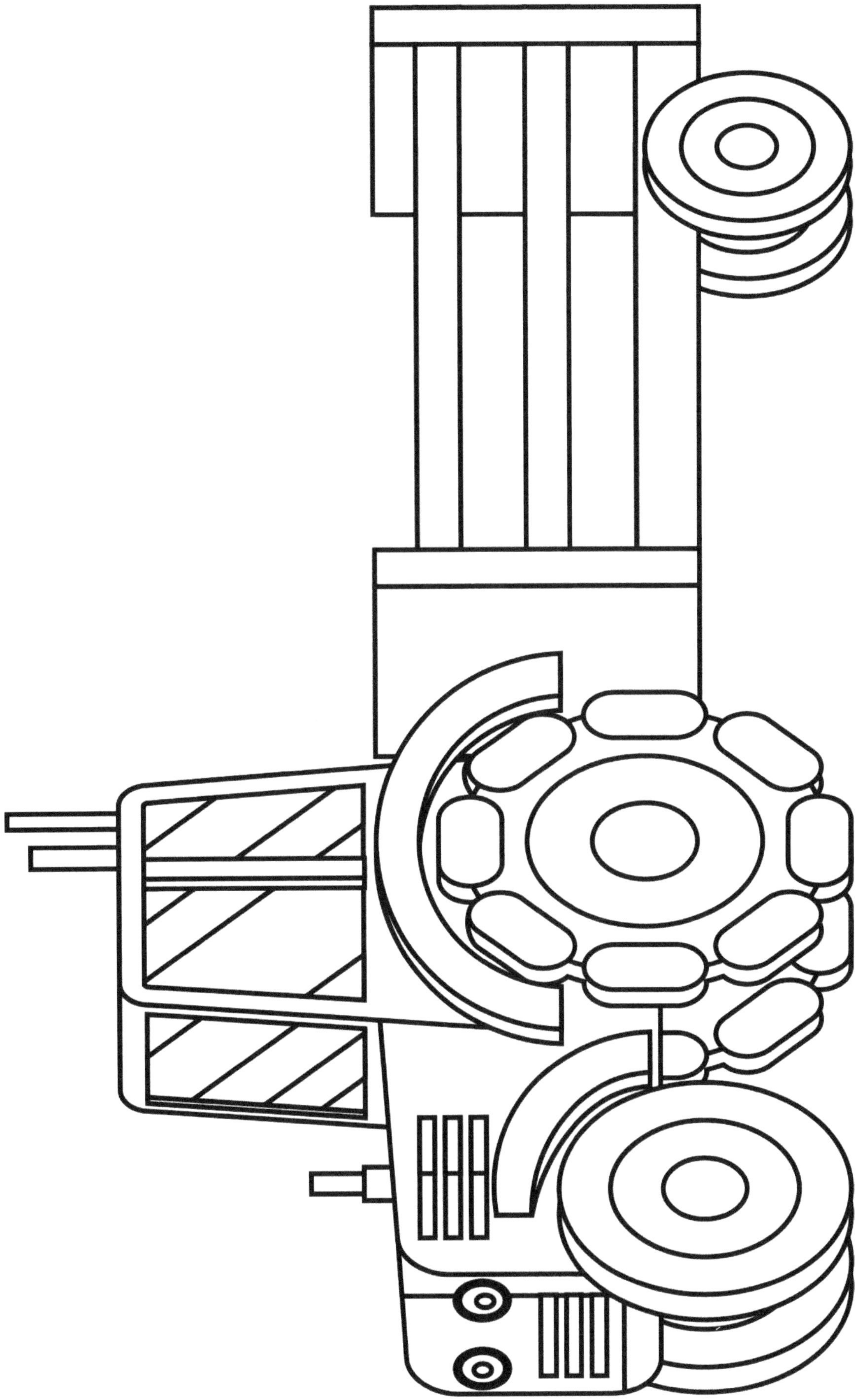

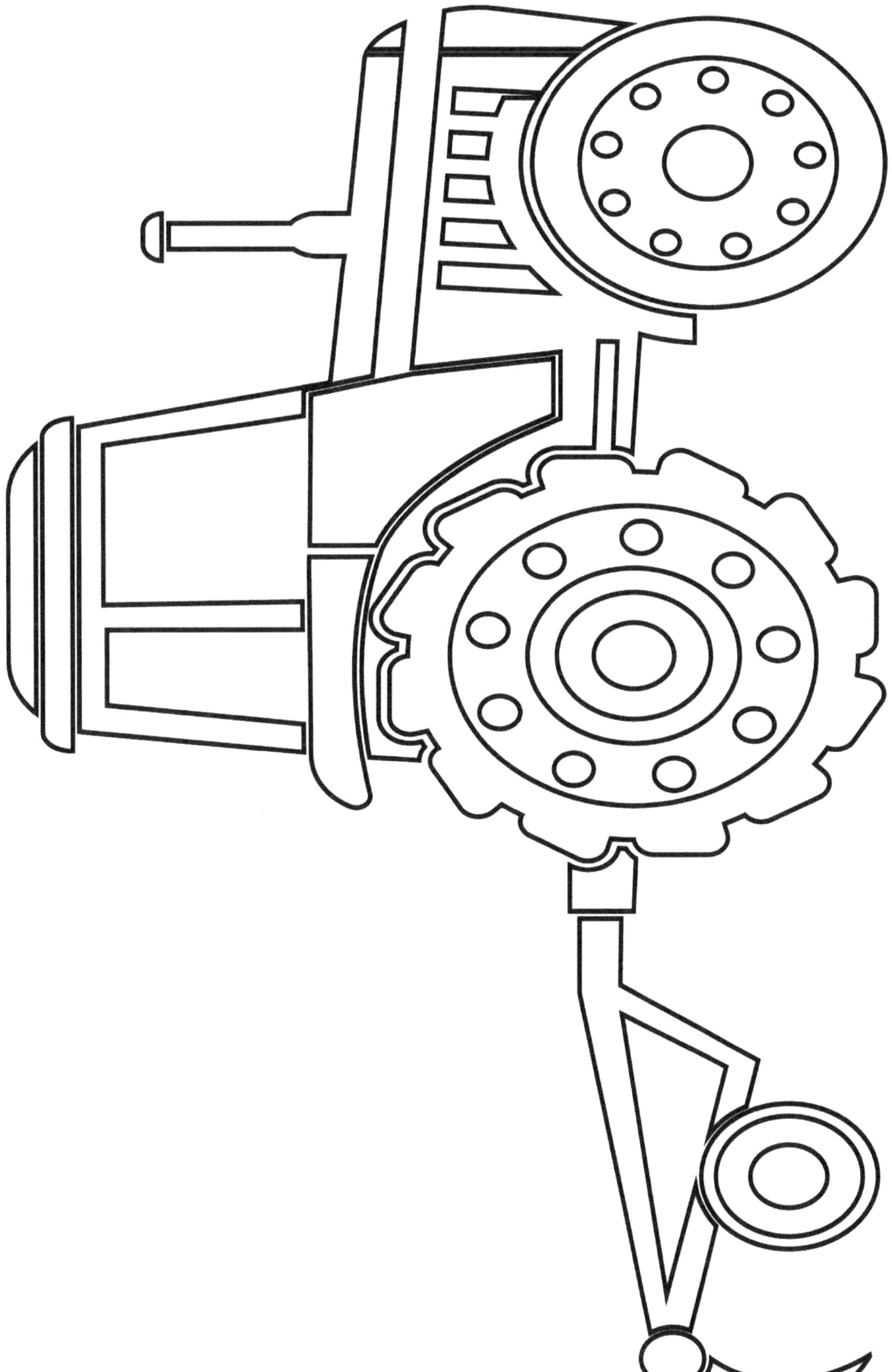

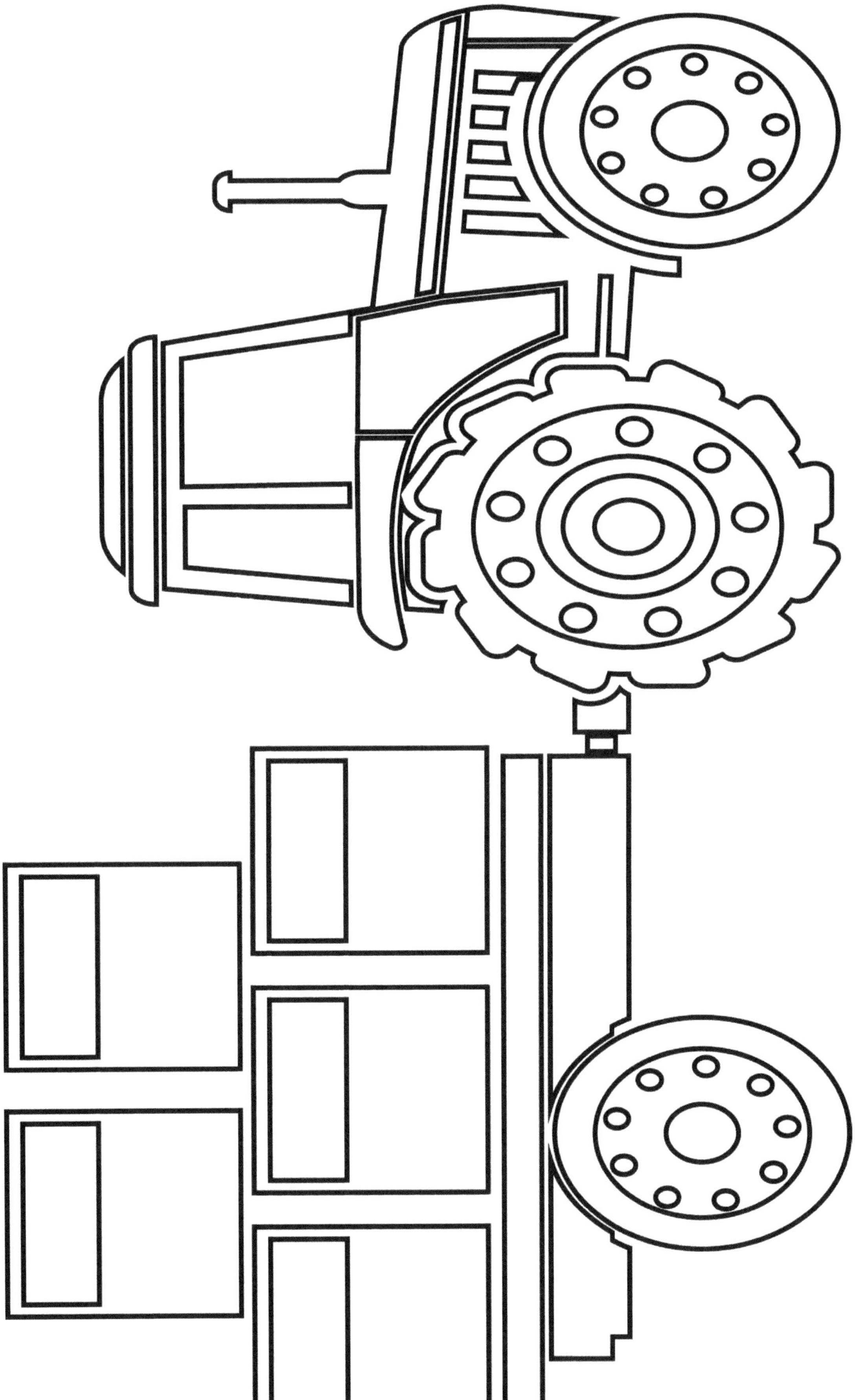

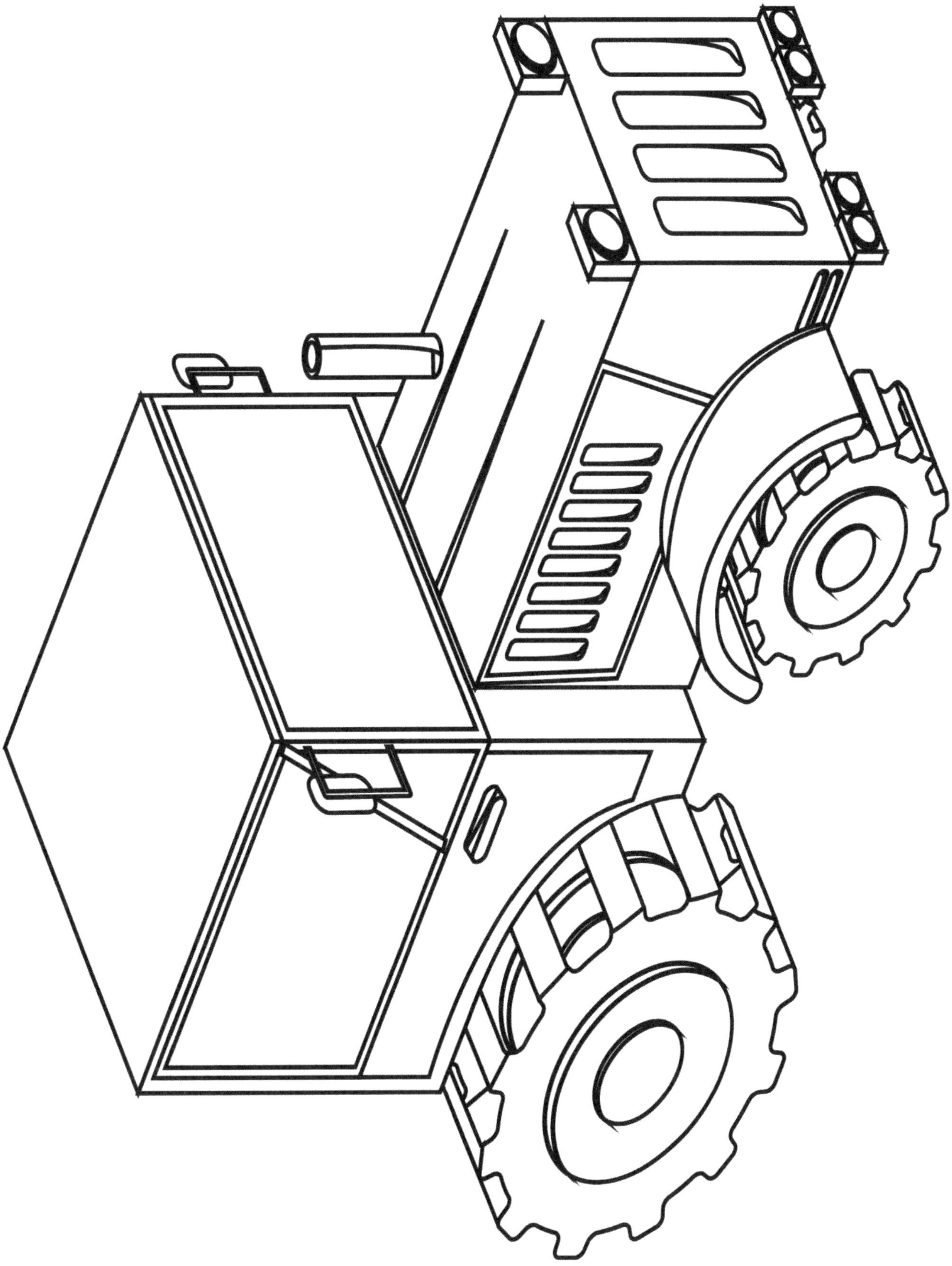

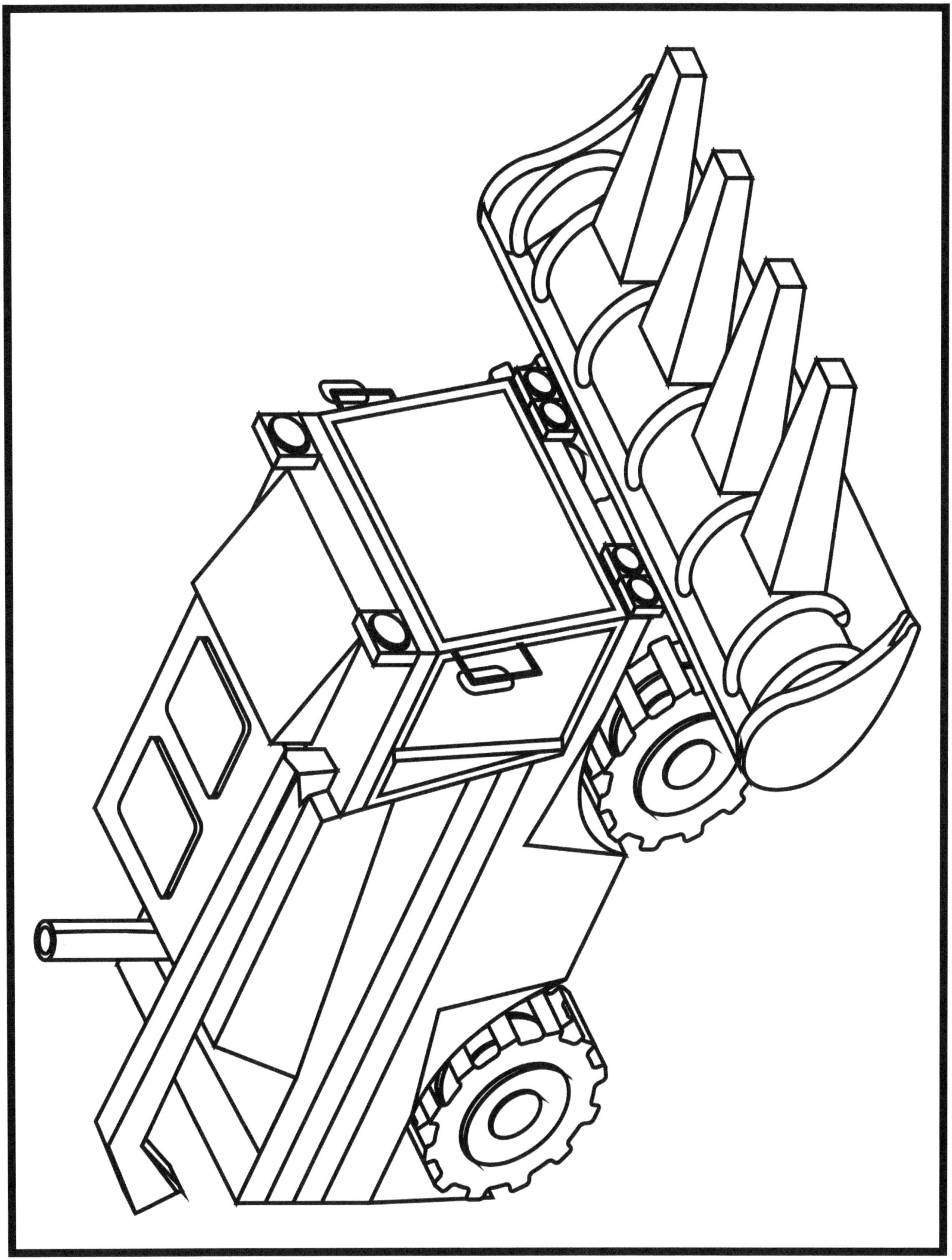

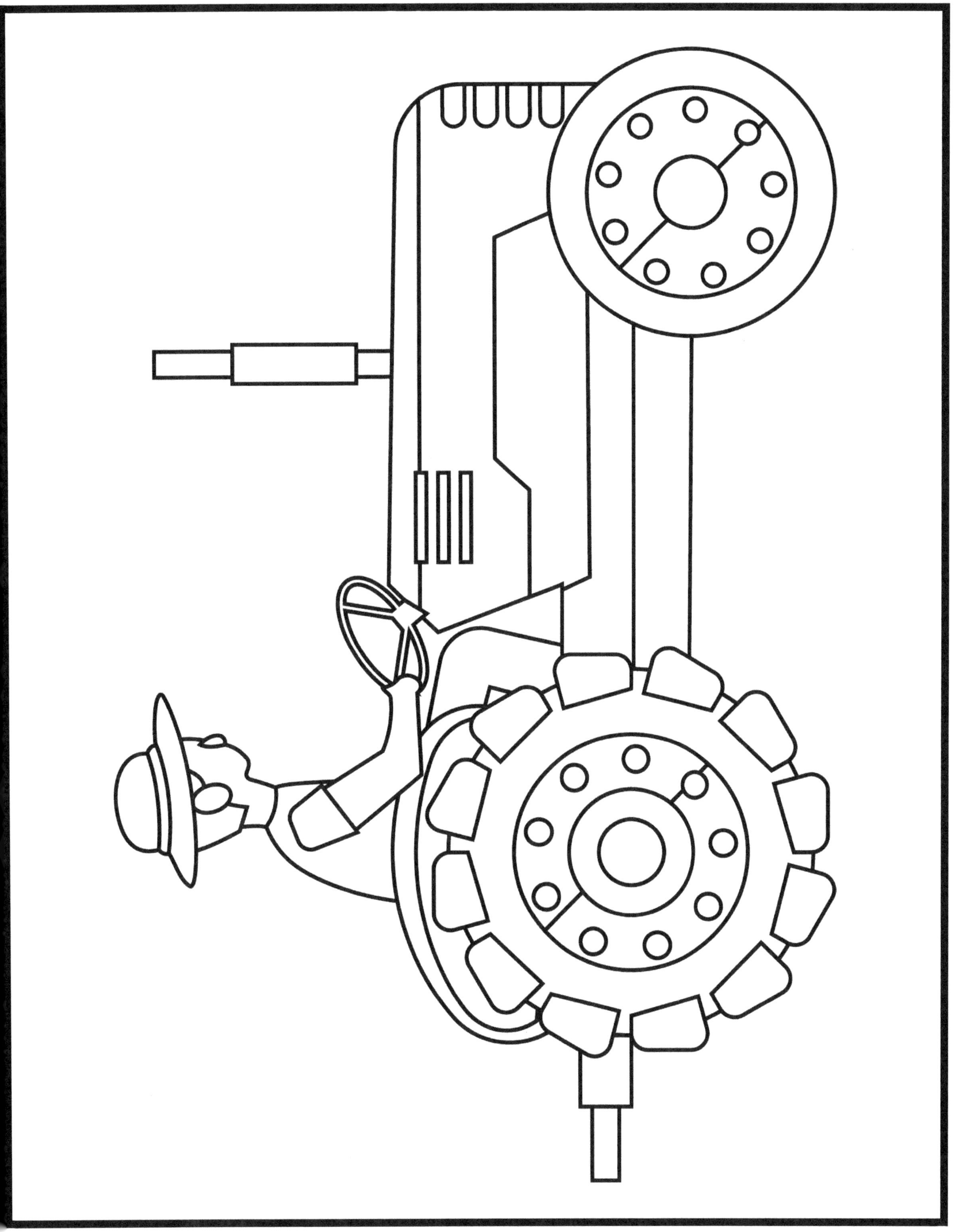

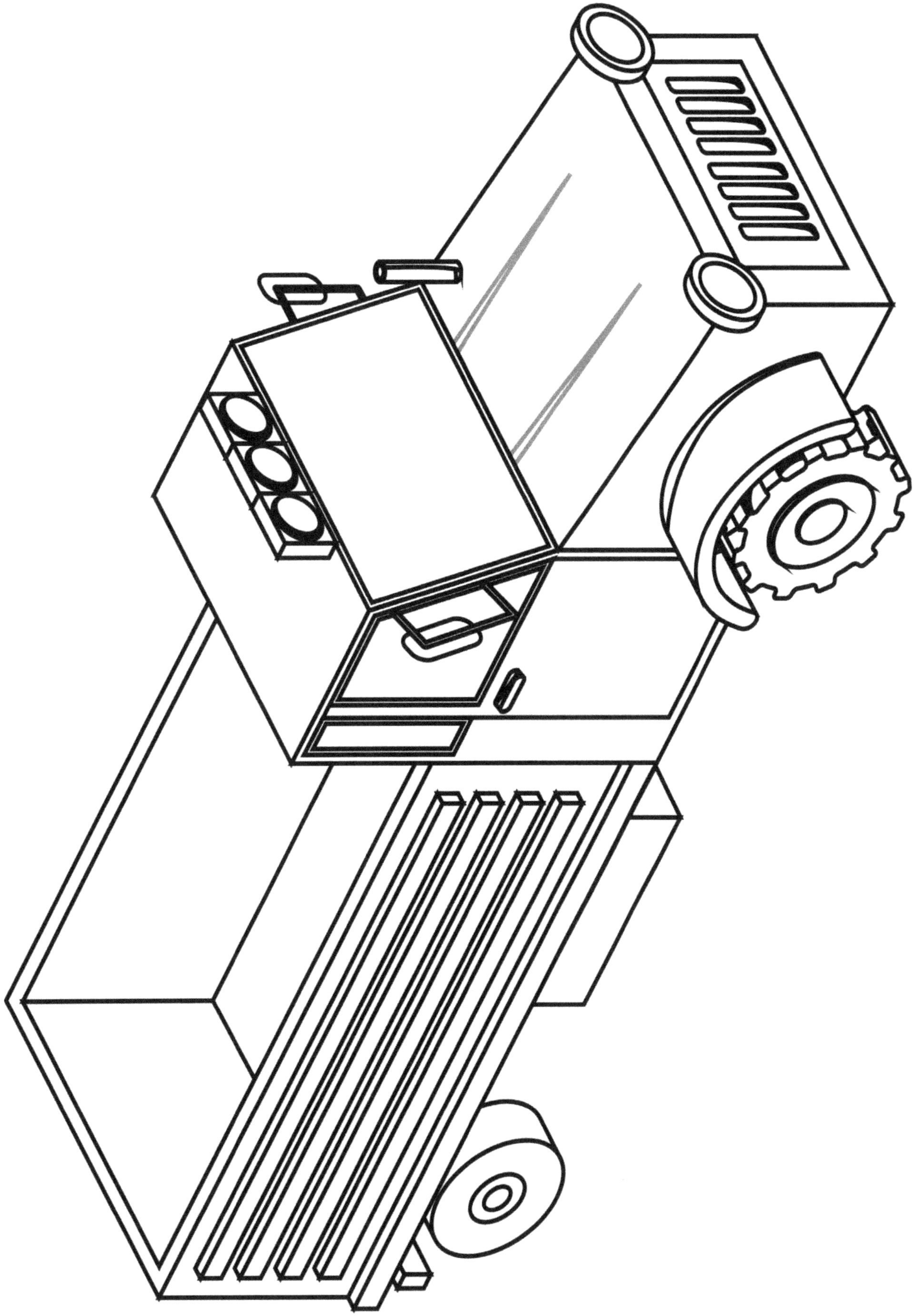

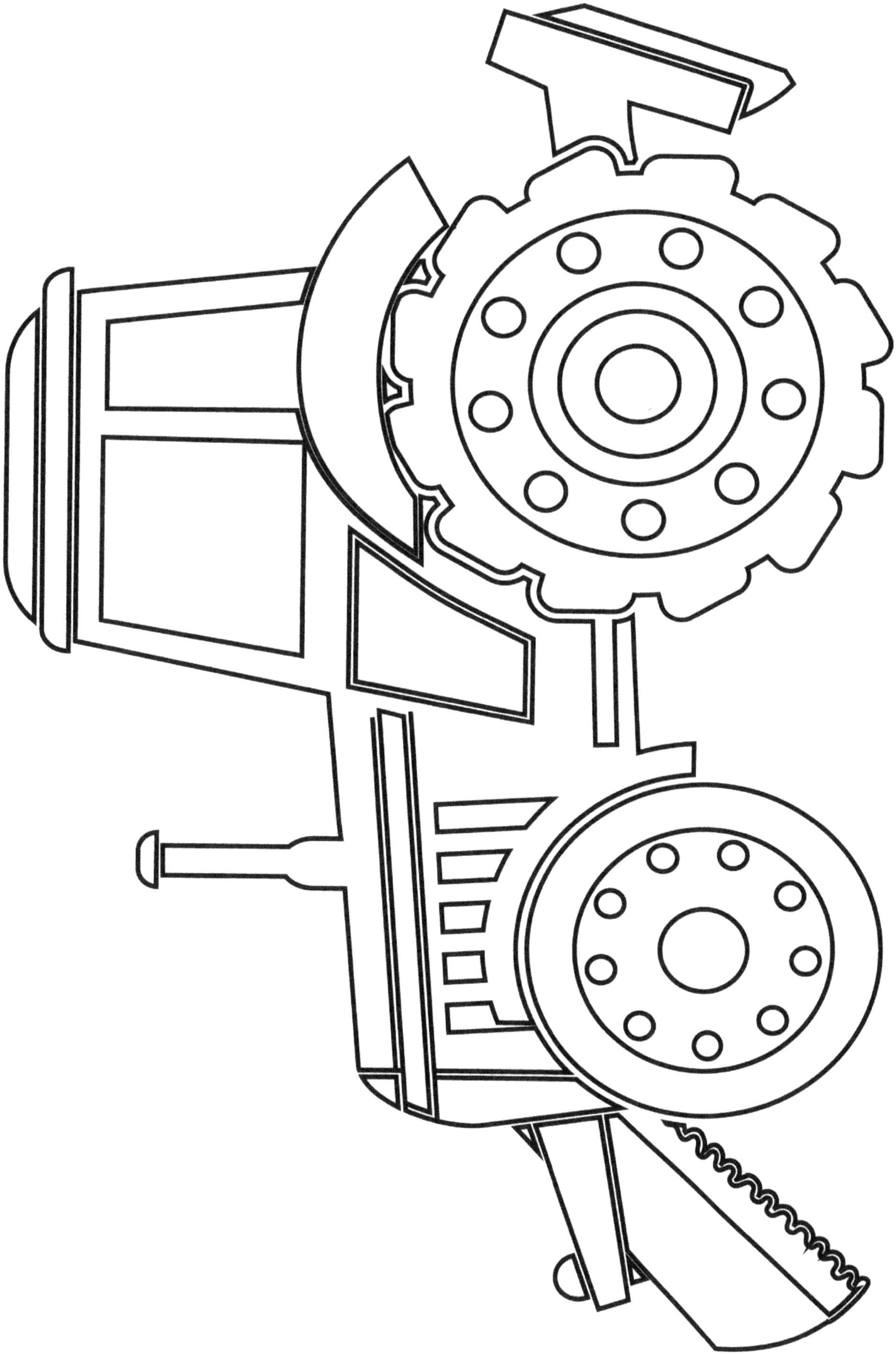

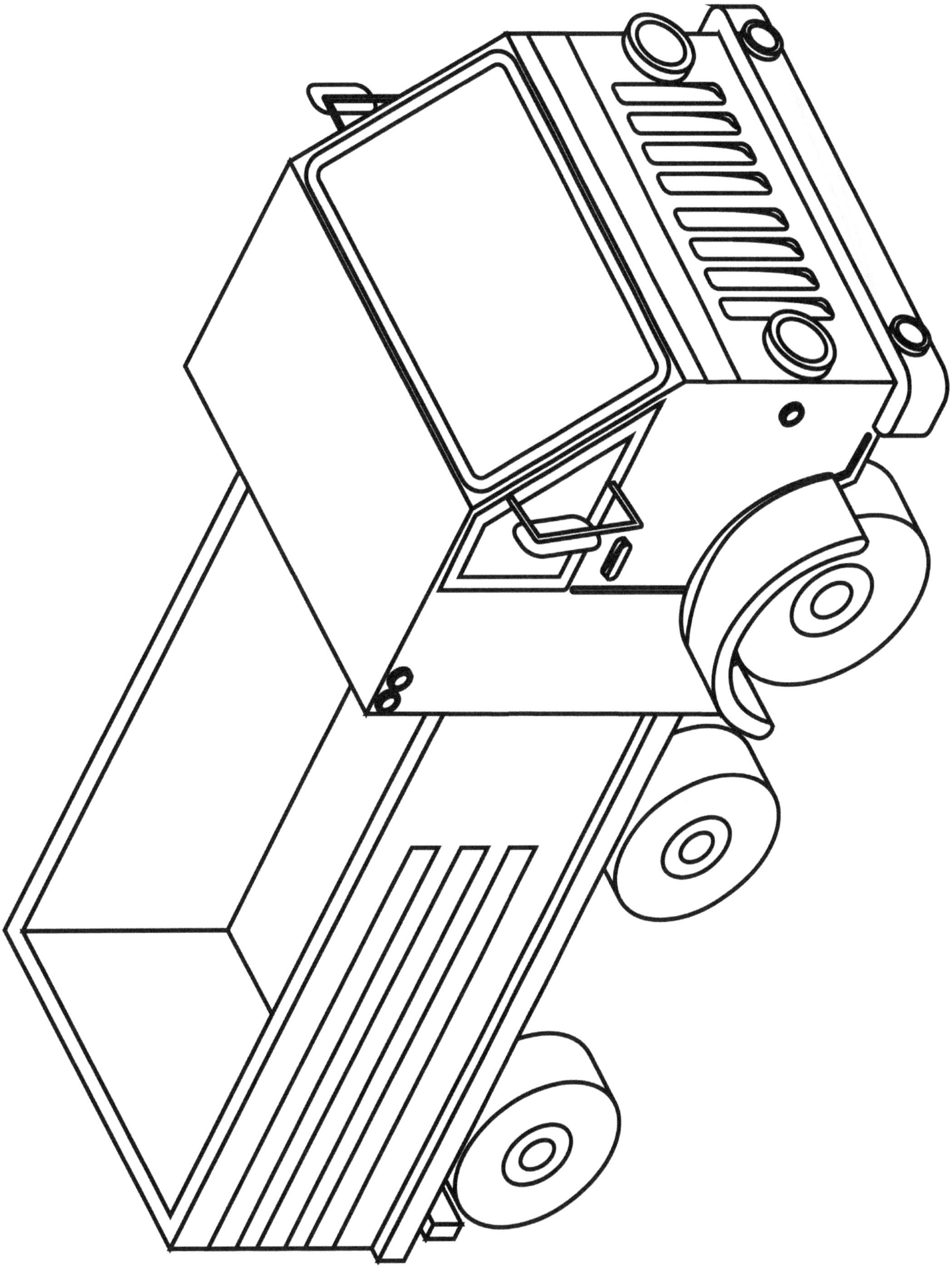

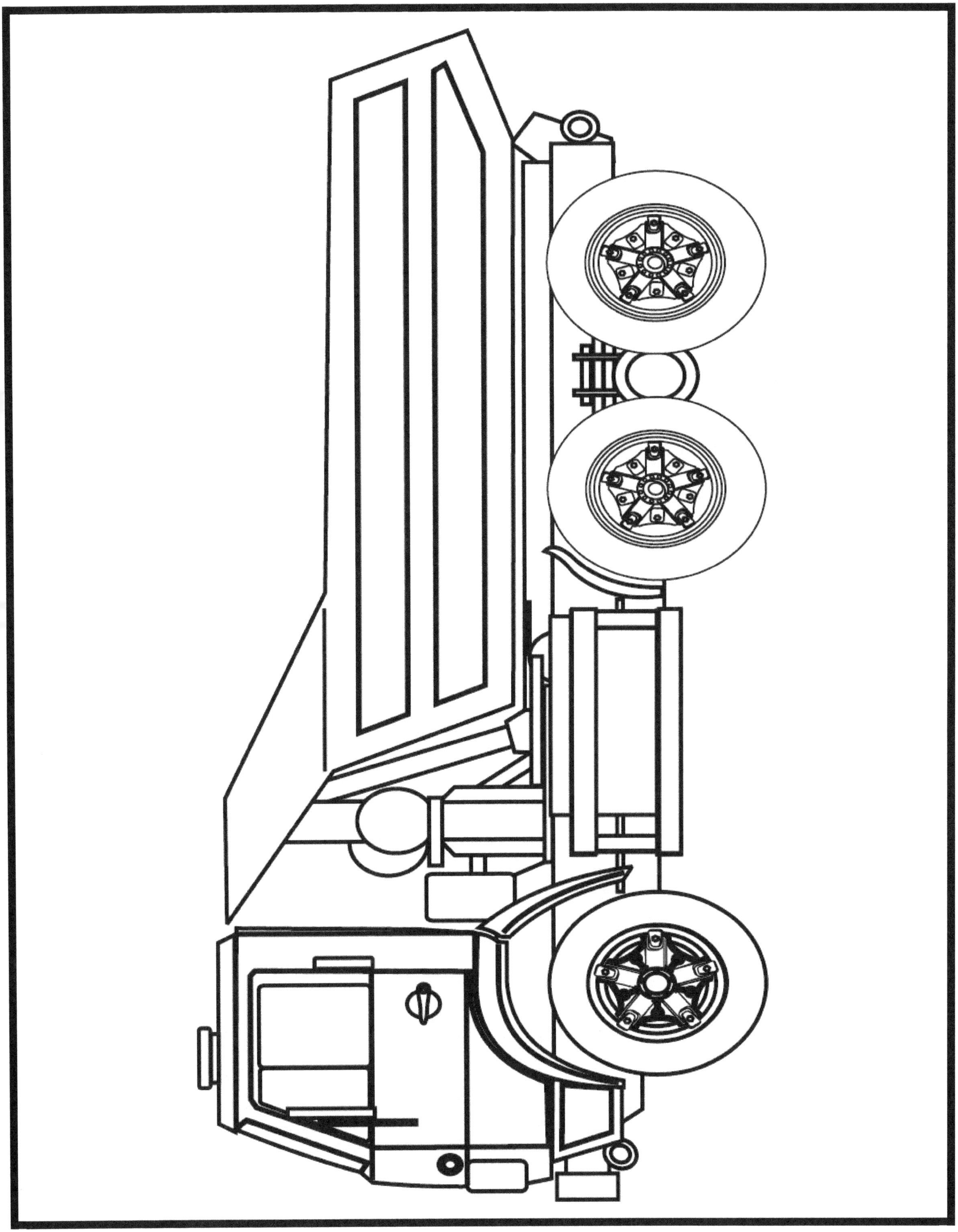

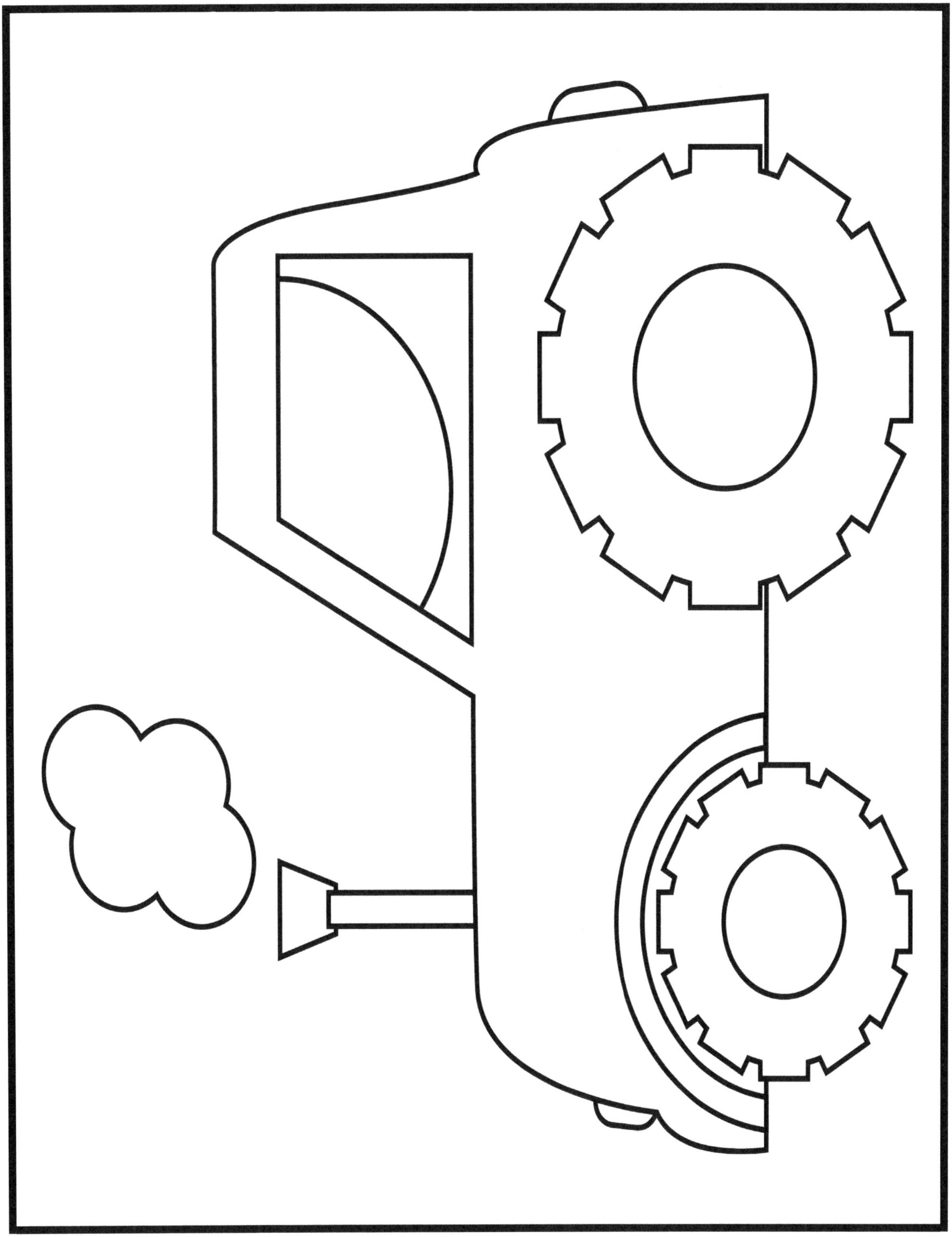

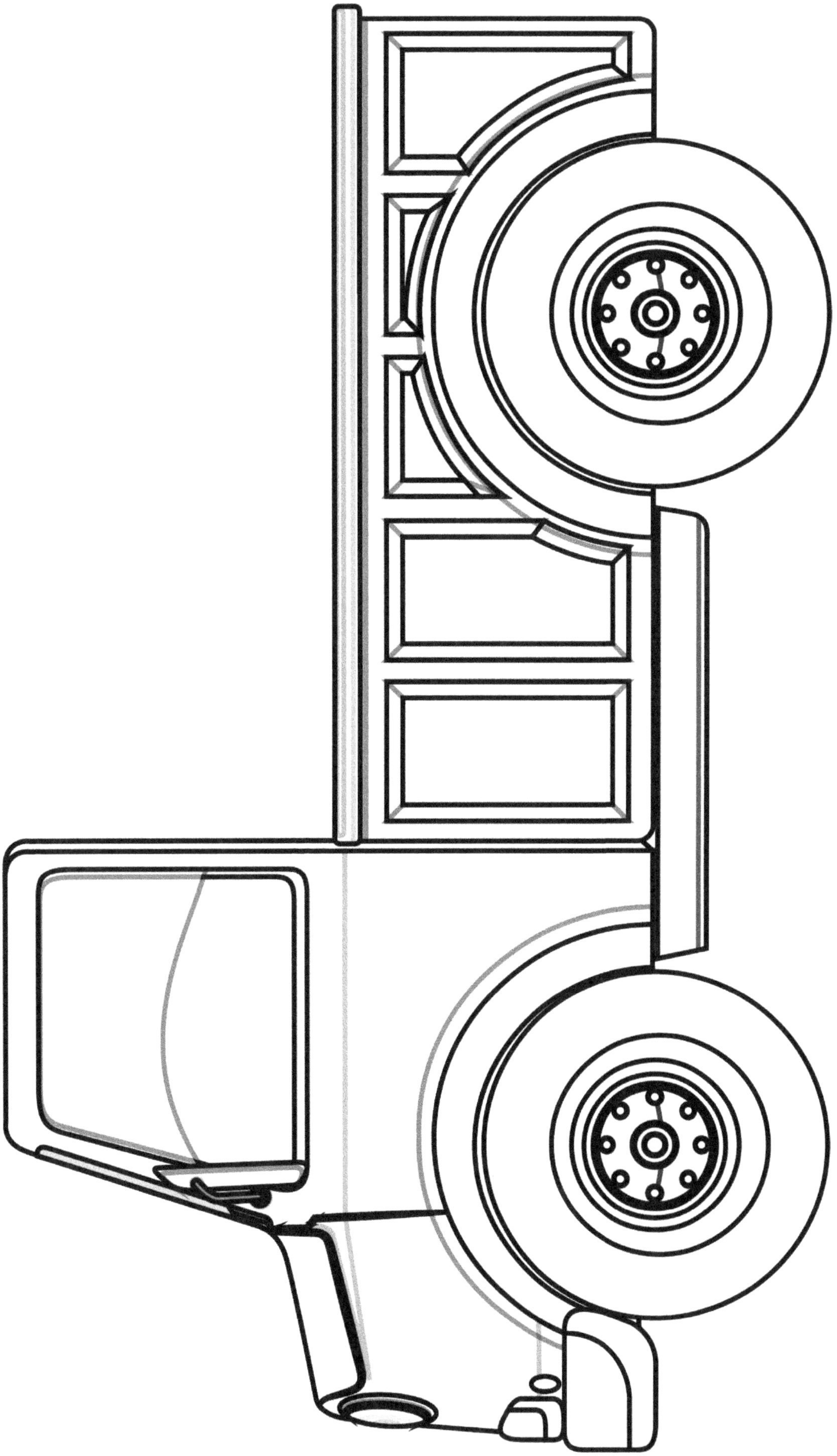

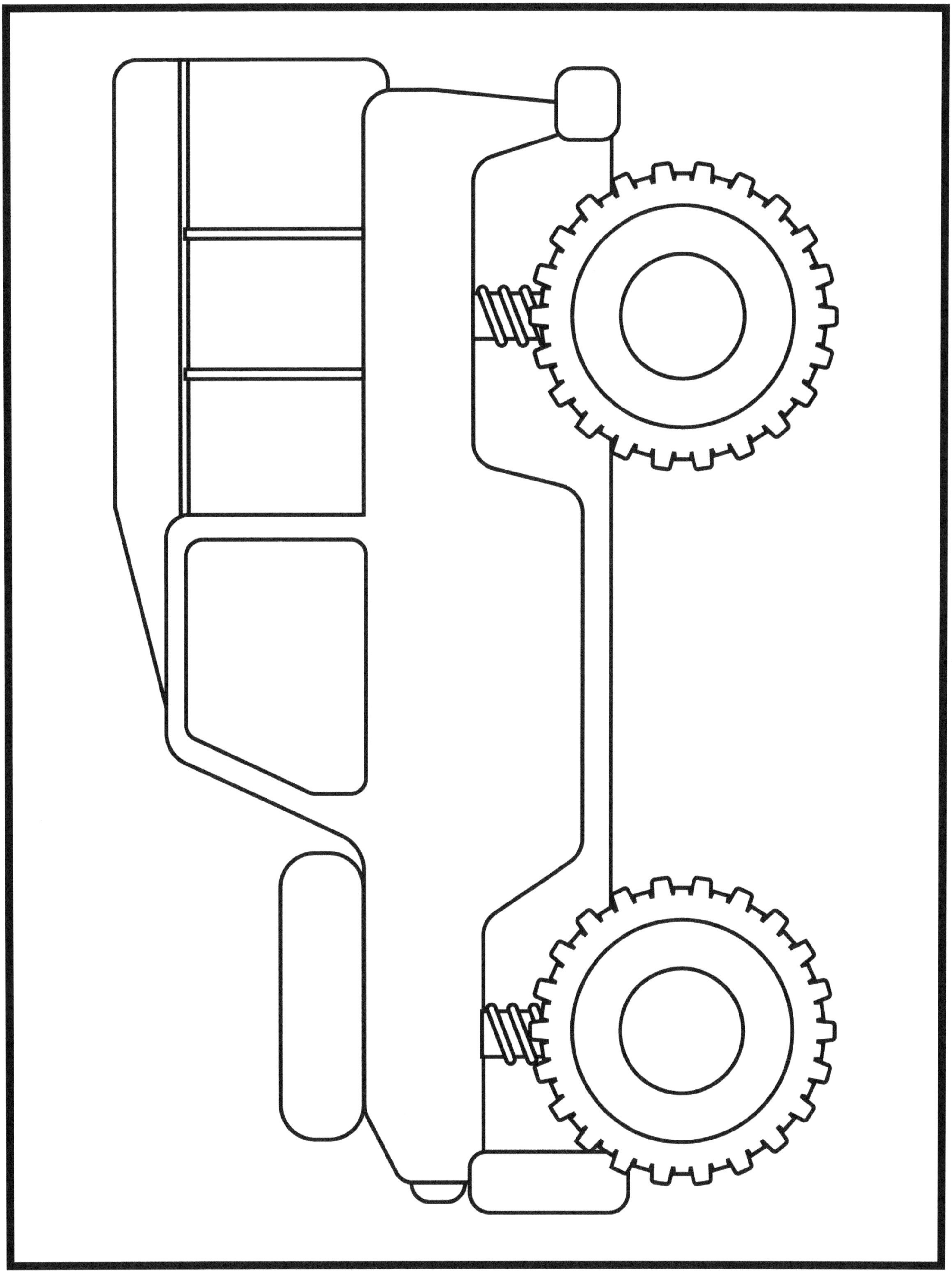

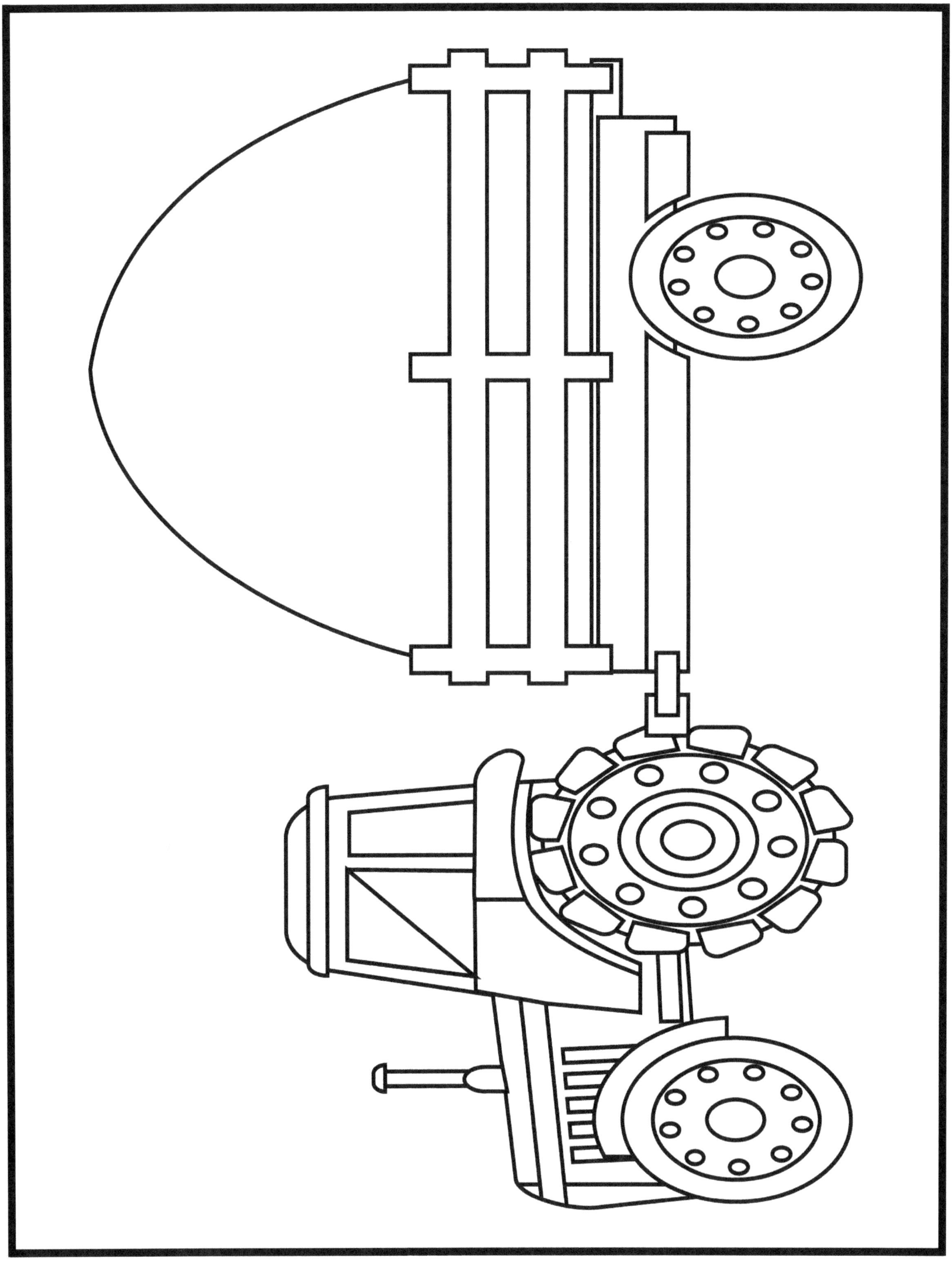

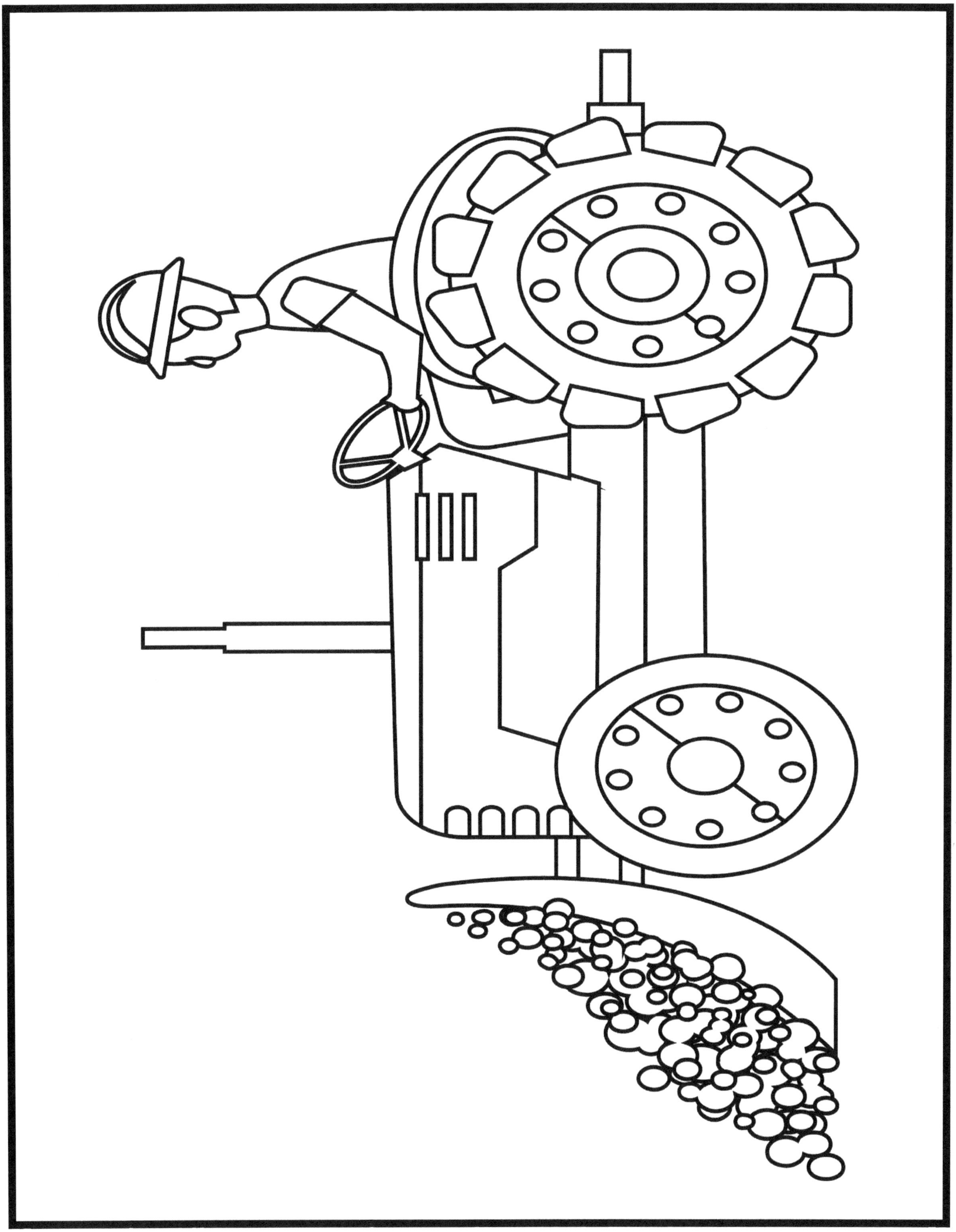

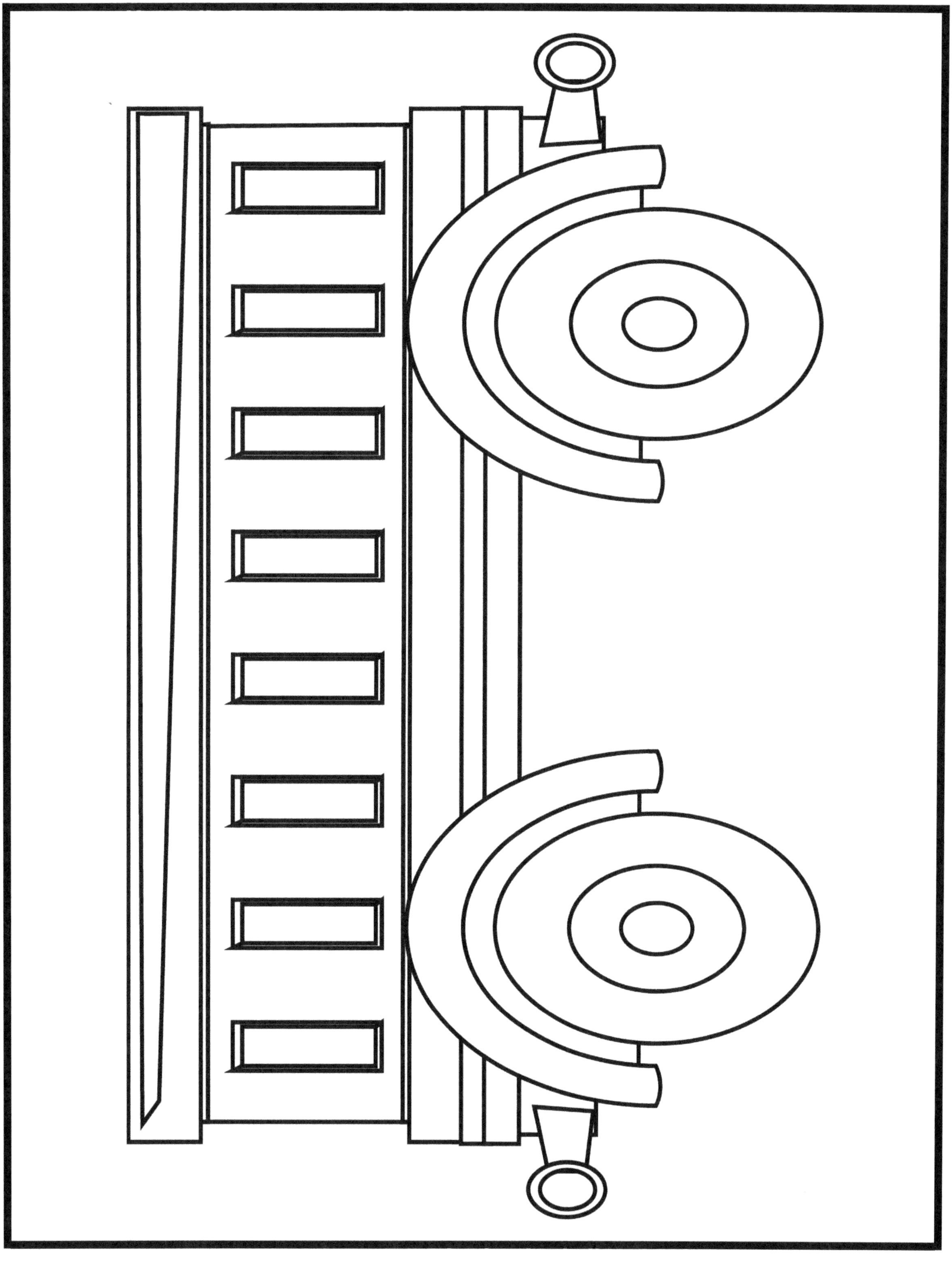

www.ingramcontent.com/pod-product-compliance
Lightning Source LLC
LaVergne TN
LVHW080930150125
801268LV00034B/1391
9798680044391